PRAIS

"Wow! I'm in complete awe. This collection left me with a heavy chest and tight throat. It's hauntingly beautiful. Sad, yet embodies hope. Divine." *Jessica Bell*

"I devoured this collection, salivated over it." *Dawn Ius*

"Great little morsels to taste and ponder. Incredible cadence." *Amie McCracken*

"Clever and bursting with imagery." *Kristen Coros*

"To say so much with so little is truly the essence of a vignette. There is simultaneously such simplicity and complexity in each piece. From beginning to end there is great tone, rhythm, and emotion throughout. The author knows just how to zero in on the specifics of an image and nail it." *Krystal A. Sital*

"Striking. Speaks volumes in such few words."
Theresa Milstein

"It is hard to overstate how much I love this. Every single word has been wrestled from a deep dark place inside the writer's soul and the result is a concision and layering that leaves a finish like the finest wine. I came back to these pieces so many times, gaining not only new insights into the human condition each time, but discovering genuinely new things about the possibilities of words."
Dan Holloway

ABOUT THE AUTHOR

Bauke Kamstra has been a visual artist for over thirty years and now paints his life experiences and the beauty around him with a different medium: words. He resides in Nova Scotia where each morning he can be found writing poetry among the trees, listening to the silence.

www.positivelywyrde.com

WE ALL REACH THE EARTH BY FALLING

ISBN-10: 0992509750
ISBN-13: 978-0-9925097-5-0

Published by Vine Leaves Press 2014
Melbourne, Vic, Australia
Athens, Attica, Greece

This is a work of fiction. Any similarity between the characters and
situations within its pages and places or persons, living or dead, is
unintentional and coincidental.

National Library of Australia Cataloguing-in-Publication entry
Author: Kamstra, Bauke, author.
Title: We all reach the Earth by falling / Bauke Kamstra.
ISBN: 9780992509750 (paperback)
Subjects: Nature--Poetry.
Dewey Number: A821.4

Cover Photography from Shutterstock.com
Cover design by Jessica Bell
Interior Design by Amie McCracken

WE ALL

REACH

the

EARTH

by

FALLING

poems

BAUKE KAMSTRA

Always I am grateful to Ellen-Louise Sutherland who provides the daily vignettes in which I live my life. Special thanks to Catherine LoFrumento-Foster, for many things, her faith & support, & whose unstinting labour & encouragement helped bring this book into being.

CONTENTS

EXERCISING
JUDGMENT

She goes into that room
beating clothes senseless
in her metal tub

she hangs them all
regardless
of their crimes

the men's shirts
flapped on the line
like chickens

until she came
and wrung their necks.

PICASSO

A tiny Picasso girl
with half grapefruit breasts
long nose
eyebrow wings

and a tiny, serious mouth

that knows
how to smile.

WISE STONES

I hold a soft stone
that with its
river weathering

has become
much smoother
than my brain

its wisdom
graces
the garden.

MUM'S ACCORDION

My mother's accordion

played so
many old hymns

but the ecstasy
was all hers.

ANDANTE

The trees a hall
but hallways end

the trees release to
          roads

          roads
do not stop
          travelling.

SONGS

Stones sing
of staying still
and loving moss

wood
of growing
slow

while flowers
open quick

and birds
carry these songs
everywhere.

RED

This blood
has come

from a wooden saint

it is as red
as a lion's tongue
and as rough.

THE THICKNESS OF WATER

The river so
swollen and sore

inflamed with wet

only summer's sun
makes this river
run thin.

SENSING

You allow me to put
my hand on your knee

the warmth
creeping up

your feelings
are often
a mystery

but not to me.

BROKEN BREADS

He learned the hard way
to break a bread

so ten could eat as four.

PRINCESS

The caravan sent
over dangerous paths

laden with banners
and precious gifts

gold and incense
silken arts

a silver script
to capture love

and return
with a princess.

THREADS

The threads come down
that were holding
us up

the birds
have also fallen

and now their shadows
are gone too.

BOX

I have a box
I've carried
all my life

never opened

I've no idea
what's inside.

GERMINATION

This poem
is in my bed
getting pregnant.

SHOE

I stack my
rows of words
and mix my mortar

ready to build
a wall

as always
there's a stone
in my shoe.

ADDER'S TONGUE

Consumed

I taste words
and ink

my tongue
has become

the nib
of a pen.

GREEN SUCCUBUS

The strange love
of ivy for walls

accumulating
generations of scars

until at last
the wall
succumbs.

STAKING TERRITORY

Men become wolves
but not with her

for she was wolf entire

looking down on them
as they cringed.

PAIN

The tree is old
dying

but I still
don't want it down

I think it's earned
its suffering

and its pieces
falling.

MOUTH

Your flesh teaches me
the mouths

that lie hidden
in my hands.

VERTIGO

In the dark blade
of your voice

my life starts
whirling

spinning me sick
and vomiting ghosts

my heart
wanting out.

BIRD WALK

Walking through the trees

a bird hopping
from pine to spruce

keeping pace

telling me
stories.

RESPECT

A few raindrops falling

some leaves dip and bow
as I pass.

DOGS & ME

A city of steps
of falling down

stray dogs
lingering
hoping

as much as you.

STATION KEEPING

Beyond the fence
the rails tiredly rust

waiting
like me
for a train.

TRADING HUNGERS

When I sleep
I wake

in the body
of a snake

peer past
the fang-folded rim
of my mouth

stretching wide
the hungry grin.

GENERATION

Prying open
the knees of my mind

exposing thoughts
and an emerging head

ideas born genderless

waiting for preferences
to kick in.

NAKED TREES

Bare branches hold
having learned stillness

while leafed ones
(still frantic)
clutch

after every passing breeze.

COMPULSION

She needs a lover
made of clay
(and dynamite)

with knotted muscles
to lift
(her)

carrying her
to the cave.

EMPTY

I remember those
children

on the street

their eyes as frequently
empty

as their mouths.

COMPARATIVE RELIGION

I see the same sun shining
on a grave

as on that girl
at the beach.

UNDER

Under the flower the bee
under the bee the honey
under the honey a queen
under the queen a jar
in the cupboard.

LOVERS

Water is just water
until you touch it

then it is a lover

just as it is
with the wind.

IKEBANA

In my sleep
(I see)

young women
(so lovely)

when I awaken
(I arrange)

cherry blossoms
(branches in a vase).

AWARENESS OF FORM

I know

it was a crow
in man-shape

the bold voice
meant to disguise

didn't hide
a scavenger's eyes.

OLD MAN

The old man walking

eyes exploding
bursts of flames

and where stick
struck earth

briars of roses
followed him.

USEFUL OBJECTS

I have no arrows
in my quiver

only the strings
of a lute

and a shell
that sounds
like water.

FIGHTING FOR HIS FAITH

His faith was as harsh
as his knuckles

swollen
scarred
and sore

a fighter's hands

this is where
he put

his greatest faith.

CONGRUENCIES

This poem is just
my inked tongue
and your paper ear.

OBSTACLES

The journey is long

the bread crumb details
long taken by birds

the roadblock
is unknown

my momentum
continuously
slows.

HAVING COME
TOGETHER

Radio music
for tasting flesh

my thumb
in her mouth

some part of her
in mine

confident signals
move us

and our familiars.

NIGHT SWEATS

The bed now reeks
of dreams

the far-realm sweat
of voyage

humid lands wait

salt rime
on the sheets.

IN THE YARD

In the yard the stones sink
grown heavy with names

the shaved lawn
pockmarked

by praying knees.

WILD GROOM

The bride went shopping
out at the farm

for wild groom

everyone knows
the free range ones

are best.

THE THINGS I HAVE

I have violins
to put in her ears

strawberries
for her mouth

and I've brought
my red tongue

should the need
(for it) arise.

NO POTATOES

I am not practical enough
for ordinary life

my feet leave the ground

in my gardens
there are no potatoes

only flowers grow.

ESSENCES

I go to the sea

I lay down my eye
and my ear

to hear the sound
that
silence would make

and see the water
as liquid diamond
would be.

SYNCHRONEITY

Music to make
a crippled man dance

living in beaks
in river rills

spilling into the house
over wooden sills.

UNEXPECTED
ENCOUNTER

I heard music
unexpectedly

behind the closed curtain

a woman's sweet laugh
fell gracefully
like the notes of a piano

so I lingered.

A DIFFERENCE OF OPINION

Two sisters
in the heat

one splits
down the middle

and becomes half
of what she was

the other does not.

FILLING ROOMS

I sat once
in an empty room
for a long time.

It was peaceful
and I was content

but I could not stay there
forever.

INDUSTRY

I've hands of bronze
but iron fists

pewter loins
and my heart, of course
is gold

my brain is mercury
swift and cold

what industry
could make use

of so much metal.

RAPTOR

In that crowd of laughing girls
he was like a hawk
borne on a fist

the girls fled
screaming.

TEA CEREMONY

The tea ceremony
separated
their desire

a shivered whisk
and ritual sip

this is the way
a furled sail

yearns the wind.

WAR POEM

I've brought you home
poems from the war

but not my leg
which died there.

FLIGHT

I walk into pigeons whose wings
argue with the air that consents
to whirl them away into trees.

FLYING FISH

I am a trout
airborne for one splashing moment
I know what it is to fly.

FOLLOWING WOODS

Walking through patches
of dark and sun

stumbling on rocks
bloodying
my wooden knees

slowly I catch up
with the movement
of trees.

VISIONARY

I walk shabby and crazed

old poets
are no longer thought

to be touched
by gods.

MOBILE

I lie on the grass

shadows painting shapes
on my chest

insects singing
clouds to rest.

WANT TO ENTER?

Submissions are open June 1 – February 28 annually.

Prize: $500 + Publication by Vine Leaves Press + 20 copies

The Vine Leaves Vignette Collection Award includes a cash prize of $500, publication by Vine Leaves Press (paperback and eBook), 20 copies of the paperback, worldwide distribution, and promotion through Vine Leaves Literary Journal and staff websites. Author will receive a 70% royalty on all eBook and print sales.

Manuscripts are judged by Vine Leaves Literary Journal staff, and a guest judge subject to change every year. This competition is open to vignettes in English (poetry and/or prose), written by authors anywhere in the world. Individual pieces in a manuscript may have been previously published in magazines, print or web journals, or anthologies, but the work as a whole must be unpublished (this includes previously self-published books.)

Employees of Vine Leaves Literary Journal are not eligible to enter.

Please visit *vineleavesliteraryjournal.com/contests* for submission guidelines.

*We are an independent, nonprofit literary journal. Submission fees help cover, though not fully, the prize money, publishing costs, and time reviewing manuscripts.

Please donate to keep our *Vine Leaves* growing...

The journal gets more than 4000 unique views a month and the compliments via email take our breaths away. Which is pretty damn excellent for a magazine running only a little over two years.

That is thanks to YOU.

But the bigger we get, the more we start to scrape the bottom of the money barrel. Especially since we are now publishing single-author vignette collections through Vine Leaves Press and offering a 70% royalty on both paperback and eBook. But this means any money that we receive goes straight back into the journal and paying contributors for their work.

Our piggy bank is running very low. We have tried to get grant support through the Australia Council for the Arts, but in order to be eligible, we would have to publish only Australian literature. We are not willing to do that. There is a world of amazing writers out there.

Can you help us?

Please do us the honour of donating a few bucks to our mission: to give the vignette, a forgotten literary form, the exposure and credit it deserves.

Just think of it as buying two coffees one morning, instead of one, for the greater good of the vignette!

www.vineleavesliteraryjournal.com/donate

Vine Leaves Press Books

We All Reach The Earth By Falling,
by Bauke Kamstra

Harvest,
by Amanya Maloba

The Best of Vine Leaves Literary Journal 2012,
edited by Jessica Bell and Dawn Ius

The Best of Vine Leaves Literary Journal 2013,
edited by Jessica Bell and Dawn Ius

Indiestructible: Inspiring Stories from the Publishing Jungle, compiled and edited by Jessica Bell

Writing in a Nutshell: Writing Workshops to Improve Your Craft, by Jessica Bell

Polish Your Fiction: A Quick & Easy Self-Editing Guide, by Jessica Bell

Forthcoming titles:

The Best of Vine Leaves Literary Journal 2014,
edited by Jessica Bell (December 1, 2014)

Cellography, by Christine Tsen (March 30, 2015)

Solace, by Colleen Mills (June 15, 2015)

Vine Leaves Literary Journal was founded to offer the vignette, a forgotten literary form, the exposure and credit it deserves.

The journal, published quarterly online, is a lush synergy of atmospheric prose, poetry, photography and illustrations, put together with an eye for aesthetics as well as literary merit. The annual print anthology showcases the very best pieces from throughout the year.

Each vignette merges to create a vivid snapshot in time and place. Prepare for big stories in small spaces, between and beyond the words.

Read one at a time.

Taste them. Savour them.

Live them.

www.vineleavesliteraryjournal.com

The best of

Vine Leaves
Literary Journal

2012

Edited by

Jessica Bell & Dawn Ius

ВИНЕТКА

VIGNETTE

The Best of
Vine Leaves Literary Journal

2013

EDITED BY JESSICA BELL & DAWN IUS

Excerpt of *HARVEST*
by Amanya Maloba
Published: July 28, 2014

SWEETNESS

My mother ate grapefruit while she was pregnant with me. She ate all that sour to balance all the sweet growing inside her. She had to wait until I was done baking before she could touch sugar again.

When she pushed me out around lunchtime, my father cut the umbilical cord and held me. He kissed my nose and said, My sweet girl, Sukari.

Later bees would attack my ripe skin placing their stingers in—an attempt to taste the blood sweeter than their honey. I cried and teachers placed the molested area in baking soda and water, explaining that the bees liked the flower scrunchie around my afro-puff.

I knew they were full of shit even then.

Lovers tell me that I taste sweet. That it's like sticking their tongue right into a honey pot and searching around for the pressure point that makes the hive explode into bits of comb and honey. Baby, you're so sweet, they always say. Those things gross men say about women don't make sense—it's nothing like the counters in the back of grocery stores, and everything like the berries growing on trees in the backyard. I never eat it though. Never have—honey or any added sugars. I gave all that up with alcohol and birth control. A body doesn't need it and with blood as sweet as mine it could kill me or turn me rancid.

Externally, honey is a cleaning product—strong enough to get rid of pimples on skin, but can turn your insides corrupt if ingested.

Keep out of reach of children, the label should say.

They're sweet enough.

Excerpt of *CELLOGRAPHY*
by Christine Tsen
Forthcoming: March 30, 2015

CELLO

Strings sprung, eyes closed, you were found
in an attic, collapsing into clutter.
How you had wingbeats for homing me
for fleeing winter's bitter whip
for warmth of fingertip's vital touch
I don't know, but like tousled hare
under towering strains of stars, we fell in love.

I know there were others before me
their full-bodied songs buried, frosted over.
They are a reminder that we have little time to warm
living out devoted days strewn with notes
crevasses reprimanding fingers to leave spaces

for silence where we both become invisible
mere channels
for the marrow of each other's bones
you in brown, my soft footed hare and I
sky winged year after year since that brief night
soundpost to the brimming of stars.

Excerpt of *SOLACE*
by Colleen Mills
Forthcoming: June 15, 2015

PART I: ASHES

There is a house with wood-stained siding,
a shale driveway lined with daffodil planter boxes,
an old oak tree and swing

and inside, my father's stove. Cast iron.
Good for drying wet innards of small shoes,
sinewy threads woven into damp socks,
the slippery cold of ice on bark.

These small, steaming piles beneath its belly
rest down memory's dark corridors
just where we left them all those years ago.

The house thick with burnt wood, wet wool, orange peels,
and waking.

The ticking of a clock.

One of my brothers pulls a flannel sheet over his head;
the other steeps his pillow full of sweat each night in the
bunk below.

I've been lying awake inside this dark hour of morning
as if I'm a doll on the stage of a small doll house,
lying very still in my bed with my eyes closed.

I imagine that I am a ghost of a child

because that is what I am: both then and now.
I am both the space around my body and the hollowness within.
I am and have always been.
I am and will always be.

A shadow of a thing. A passing over. The knowing of absence,
of being only two watching eyes shifting beneath slits in the flesh.

Down the hallway my father sits in the living room
reading the paper from his armchair,
feet extended, TV news on repeat—

        underwear,
      socks pulled to the ankle,
      a work shirt open at the collar.

This is how my memory returns to him,
returns in the quiet moments between thoughts,
returns on a small whisper of air sucked sharply through the lips.

The heart knows well that it can only forget
the things it never really cared about.

CPSIA information can be obtained
at www.ICGtesting.com
Printed in the USA
BVHW01s1617150118
505275BV00017B/547/P